Printed in the United States of America
First Printing 2016
ISBN 978-0-9965556-2-3

Firefly Grace Publishing
Burlington, VT 05403
www.EmilyRLong.com

Interior and Cover Design: ShiftFWD

INTRODUCTION

Oh, Mama. I am so very sorry.

I am so sorry that your arms are empty and your heart, so filled with love for your precious, irreplaceable child, has been broken and battered with grief.

If you were here with me now, I would wrap my arms around you and simply hold on while you cried the seeming endless tears and wailed for the terrible longing in your soul to be with your child. I would be there, standing or sitting or laying with you, so that you would know in every moment that you are not alone and that you are loved. I would bring you hot cocoa or tea and warm cookies and listen to you talk about your beloved baby as long as you needed. When you needed a distraction from the heavy weight of grief and longing, I would tell you outrageous silly stories and tug you outside to walk in the sunshine and the trees in a world that, even while it feels it shouldn't, is continuing to move and live.

I desperately wish I could do this with every heartbroken and grieving mama in the world. Unfortunately, I can't. The next best thing I feel I can do is to bring this book to life and put it out into the world for you to find – a simple and sweet collection of words and love from me and other mamas like me, and like you, who are missing our deeply loved babies.

This is a book that you can hold, in those dark, lonely and desperate moments of grief and pain and loss. A book you can open to any page and read the love-filled words of another mama like you who knows the pain of not being able to hold or see or hear the one you love most in the world. A reminder in the midst of grief and tears that you are not alone and you are loved.

My hope is that this book has a little something for everyone – the letters within it's pages come from mamas with different backgrounds, different experiences, and different belief systems. Not all of them will be an exact fit for what you are experiencing, but each hold unfaltering love and a desire to reach out from heart to heart. Some of the letters included here might not fit what you believe or know to be true for yourself, but perhaps even in those, there may be a line or a phrase that is exactly what your aching heart needs to hear in this moment. If not, you can simply move on to another letter that may hold the words that your heart is seeking to hear and know.

These words and letters are written from our hearts to yours, from one mother to another. With open arms and big hearts, we welcome you (though we desperately wish we didn't have to) to our tribe of sisters – the community of mothers who know this unspeakable loss and grief. More importantly than the loss, however, we know the same beautiful mother love that lives in your heart – deep and abiding love for the child you cannot hold or see or hear yet who lives in your heart each and every moment.

It is my hope that within these pages you will find love and bits of comfort. It is my hope that you will feel, deep down into your bones, that you are not alone and that you are so very loved. It is my hope that you will know without a doubt that your baby and your motherhood matter. It is my hope that you will know that your baby's life, however brief, has touched this world in irrevocable and valuable ways.

And so, with all my love and all my hopes, I offer you this simple book filled with love and letters from our hearts to yours.

You are not alone.
You love and you are loved.

And love never dies.

LOVE LETTERS

From Our Hearts to Yours

DEAR BEREAVED MOTHER,

I know that you wish this wasn't addressed to you. I know that you wish "Bereaved Mother" was not a title that now described you. Oh, how I have wished the same. It is simply another reminder of the unfairness of it all. It is not fair that the beautiful title of "Mother" is now forever tainted with that qualifier. I am so, so sorry. I am so sorry for the loss of your precious child (or children). Nothing about this is fair. It is not fair for a mother to bury her child, or to lose a child before they have even begun to grow. It is not fair that loved and dearly wanted children are lost every single day.

I know that you are in so much pain. The pain of child loss truly is like no other. It is a pain that can only come from losing that which came from you -- your own flesh and blood, your sweet child, taken far too soon. I know your heart has been shattered, but I can tell you this -- it is not broken beyond repair. You must now begin the heavy task of picking up the pieces. The process will be slow, but take all the time you need. As you begin to rebuild your shattered life, know that there are no rules. You can choose which pieces you pick back up. If something (or someone) no longer serves you, let it go. You will quickly learn, if you haven't already, that people will change drastically after you experience such a terrible loss. Some will simply disappear; others will pretend that nothing has happened. Some will try to be supportive, but in all the wrong ways. And a few (maybe even just one) will embrace you as you are now, allow you to grieve (even grieve with you), and will be there for you no matter what road you choose to take. Surround yourself with these people, whether they live nearby, or are simply a face on your computer screen.

And lastly, allow yourself to feel whatever it is you are feeling at the moment. The grief you now carry has no expiration date. For as long as there is love, there will be grief, and that is okay.

With love,

Alex Hopper, Cyrus' mommy

To read Cyrus' story please visit: www.hopeintheheartache. wordpress.com

"FOR AS LONG AS THERE IS LOVE, THERE WILL BE GRIEF, AND THAT IS OKAY."

MY DEAR LOSS MOTHER,

I'm so, so sorry. I'm sorry this is now part of your life. I'm sorry for the daily pain, the triggers, the reminders of what should have been and what you don't have. I'm sorry that your heartbreak mirrors my own broken heart. I'm sorry we both now walk this path of grief. Yet, we BOTH walk it, you do not walk it alone. Please allow my broken heart to welcome your broken heart, to the best-worst community in the world. Here, we speak and understand the language of the bereaved and the broken – we are fluent in grief. We, your fellow Loss Mothers', we understand all too well.

We understand sadness, anger, unfairness, jealousy. We understand triggers and the bittersweet flashbacks and memories that both hurt us and heal us. I understand that every crack on your heart is there because of love; a love so deep, so strong, so durable it supersedes death. I understand that despite the pain, losing them was worth the pain – the privilege of loving them far exceeds the heartbreak of losing them.

I know what it is like to walk around this earth raw. Raw and exposed, feeling as if I didn't have any skin – each and every nerve ending grieving – to my very core. I'm here to tell you, with time, the rawness fades. You will grow a new skin, a different skin. It will be a reflection of your experiences in life and grief, just like a mosaic, there is beauty in our brokenness.

I, also, have been haunted by the Whys – why me? Why him? Why us? I've faced the injustice and watched others get to parent their babies and raise their children, while I visit the cemetery. I've not sorted out all the answers to the Whys, but I have learned – I was taught by another Loss Mother – the critical piece that keeps me sane. I was taught that my baby's life mattered; he was here, he was loved and his life is and was important. My baby made me who I am today, he made me a mother. His death made me a bereaved mother; both his existence and his passing changed me on a cellular level.

How I see and experience life is very different now. I'm grateful for every hug, every 'I love you' and I recognize how precious the smallest of moments are.

My broken heart greets your broken heart and I honour the shattered parts of you that mirror the shattered parts of me. In my heart, I hold space for you and your child and recognize and share the immense love you have for them. I see them, I honour them and I will remember them with you.

Love,

Andrea Manning

"I UNDERSTAND THAT EVERY CRACK ON YOUR HEART IS THERE BECAUSE OF LOVE; A LOVE SO DEEP, SO STRONG, SO DURABLE IT SUPERSEDES DEATH. I UNDERSTAND THAT DESPITE THE PAIN, LOSING THEM WAS WORTH THE PAIN – THE PRIVILEGE OF LOVING THEM FAR EXCEEDS THE HEARTBREAK OF LOSING THEM."

DEAR NEWLY BEREAVED MOTHER,

This will likely be the hardest thing you'll ever do. Survive this. And eventually, thrive again.

At times it will feel virtually impossible. You'll wonder how a human being can survive such pain. You'll learn you know how to defy the impossible. You've been doing it from the very moment your child's heart stopped, and yours kept beating. You do it with every breath and step you take. You're doing it now. And now. And now.

Your fingernails will become bloodied from clawing your way from the depths of despair. Your spirit will grow weary from fighting to survive. Your eyes will cry more tears than you ever thought possible. Your arms will ache an ache for which there are not words. For a lifetime.

Your heart will break into a million tiny pieces. You'll wonder how it will ever mend again.

But with every morsel of unspeakable pain, there is love. An abundance of love. A love so strong, so powerful, it will buoy you. You will not drown.

Others will say things that are intended to be helpful, but aren't. Take what is, leave what isn't.

Still, you'll meet others along the journey who will get it

without ever saying a word. Kind souls who will breathe you back to life again. Let them.

Years down the road you'll tire of hearing the same advice and clichés, over and over again. Advice that you don't want or need. Everyone will try to tell you how to best "fix" your broken heart. The trouble is, you don't need fixing.

There is no fix for this.

Eventually you'll learn how to carry the weight of this pain. At times it will crush you. At other times you'll learn how to shoulder the burden with newfound grit and grace. Either way, you'll learn how to bend with the weight of it.

It will not break you. Not entirely.

And even if you don't believe in hope – not even a little – hope will light the way for you. At times you won't realize your path is lit. The darkness feels all consuming when you're in it. But know the light is there. Surrounding you now. And now. And now.

Know you're being guided, by all of us who have survived this impossible hell. You may not hear us, or see us, but we are with you. Beside you. Hand in hand, heart to heart. Always. Just like your child still is.

Above all else, know that no one can save you but yourself.

You are the heroine/hero of this sad story. You are the one who gets to decide how, and if, you'll survive this. You are the one who will figure out a way to survive the sleepless nights, and the endless days. You are the one who will decide if and when you'll find a purpose again that means something to you. You are the one who will choose how you'll live with the pain. You are the one who will decide what you'll to cling to, what will make your life worth living again. You, and only you, get to decide how you'll survive.

No one else can do this for you.

People will speak of "closure," of "moving on," of "getting over it," of grief coming to an end. Smile kindly, and know, anyone who says these things hasn't lived this thing called grief.

To lose a child is to lose the very heart and soul of you. It is overwhelmingly disorienting. It takes a long, long time to find yourself again. It takes a long time to grow new life around the chasm of such grave loss. It takes a long time to grow beauty from ashes.

There will always be a hole in your heart, the size and shape of your child. Your child is absolutely irreplaceable. Nothing will fill the void they left. But your heart will grow bigger – beautifully bigger – around the empty space your child left behind.

The love and pain you carry for your precious child will be woven into every thread of your being. It will fuel you to things you never dreamed you could do.

Eventually, you'll figure out how to live for both of you. It will be beautiful, and it will be hard.

But, the love you two share will carry you through. You will spread this love everywhere you go.

Eventually, you'll be able to see again. Eventually, you'll find your way again. Eventually you'll realize you not only survived.

Somehow, you even thrived.

Love,

Angela

www.abedformyheart.com
www.facebook.com/abedformyheart

(Originally published on Still Standing Magazine – www. stillstandingmag.com)

"KNOW YOU'RE BEING GUIDED, BY ALL OF US WHO HAVE SURVIVED THIS IMPOSSIBLE HELL. YOU MAY NOT HEAR US, OR SEE US, BUT WE ARE WITH YOU. BESIDE YOU. HAND IN HAND, HEART TO HEART. ALWAYS. JUST LIKE YOUR CHILD STILL IS."

DEAR FELLOW LOSS MAMA,

What follows in this letter is a timeline of grieving. A trajectory of pain after the death of my son Anderson at 26 days old, as I cycled through my own stages of grief in a way that you may recognize and so come to know that you are not alone.

The first year: I am exhausted. I figured I'd have plenty of time to meet other mommy-friends in my new city when I had a baby in tow. Now, baby-less, I'm having trouble engaging in the act of living. I hate how I look with all my muscle tone gone, but the thought of the work to get it back is just exhausting. I crave junk food, especially carbs and chocolate, and I let myself have them because I'm still underweight and I'm grieving and even my grief book says to let myself eat whatever I find comforting for a while.

I wonder: am I still me? I used to be optimistic; now I'm fatalistic. I used to be emotionally steady; pre-Ander, I could not tell you the last time I had cried. Now, I know it was two days ago. And the day before that. Worst of all are the mood swings, when I get into funks, deep, depressing swings of the pendulum where I want to be morose and unhelpful and quiet and do nothing. It's hard work to get out of those grief cycles, and much of the time, I don't want to put forth the effort. At the same time, I hate that I'm not "living my life to the fullest" and appreciating what I have. I go running because I know it's good for me, not because I want to anymore. I think that someday, the wanting will come back. Until then, on the bad days, when the old me seems to have gone to an alternate universe, I fake it 'til I make it.

This strategy works for me. The second year, I rejoin life. I will always be a Babyloss Mama, but I don't want that to be my dominant identity. I need something else. I set the intention to be someone who Lives.

Exactly two years after my son's death, the grief is so much less sharp than it was before that at times I feel guilty. I still think of him every day, and likely always will, but the edges have blunted tremendously. I both hate that, and am grateful for it. I miss my little boy, but living has gotten easier. I can no longer remember when I last cried. I enjoy taking kickboxing classes and I'm eating healthfully. Time and hard grief work helped me find the motivation to be the woman and mother I wanted to be. It will get better for you, too, but be kind and gentle with yourself until it does.

Love,

Caitlin

https://babylossmama.wordpress.com

"TIME AND HARD GRIEF WORK HELPED ME FIND THE MOTIVATION TO BE THE WOMAN AND MOTHER I WANTED TO BE. IT WILL GET BETTER FOR YOU, TOO, BUT BE KIND AND GENTLE WITH YOURSELF UNTIL IT DOES."

MY SOUL SISTER,

I see you walking in my footsteps and my heart hurts with yours, Mama. How I wish I could stand by your side and hold your hand . . . hear about your baby and share your memories. But all I have are words, and I suck at writing inspiring letters. I wish I was better, especially today, and especially for you, because you deserve the best and you need hope and inspiration. But there are a few things I can share with you, and I hope they will help, these small pieces of advice from your sister in grief. I won't lie, I know it won't help much. The only thing you need is to have your baby back, and I can't do that for you. But maybe this can help you a little bit - let's aim for a little bit.

A dead baby is still a baby. Your sweet baby is not in a box. He is not lost, how could he? You were taking such good care of him. He is not even gone. You carry him, always. He goes with you, everywhere. He is still your child. You are still a mother, his mother. Death didn't change that. Nothing could change that. Remember it when you feel everyone is forgetting. Remember it when you feel you are forgetting yourself.

You can speak your baby's name. Maybe your friends and family will be afraid to talk about your baby. Maybe they won't speak the beautiful name you chose for your child, because they'll be afraid to make you sad or to remind you. My soul sister, I know you're already sad, and I know you could never forget. You don't have to take their lead. Never be afraid to speak your baby's name.

You're not mean, you're grieving. My baby Soley died from a brain cancer when she was 11 months. She fought hard, but there was no cure. Grieving her didn't make me grow as a person - this is real life, not Eat Pray Love. It didn't turn me into a kinder, stronger, more compassionate person. No - it broke me in a million pieces and made me angry, and jealous, and hopeless, and bitter. So if you feel the same, at least now you know there are two of us.

People's reactions to death suck. You don't. I've found dealing with other people's reactions to my loss (the stupid comments, the selfishness, the isolation) to be one of the hardest parts of grief. I was hurt and angry every time I got the usual "at least you're young, you can have another one" or "she was very sick, maybe it's for the best." I couldn't brush it off, and I would keep on thinking about it afterward, like I had failed my daughter somehow. Like something was wrong with me. But this had nothing to do with me - the truth is that people are uneducated about grief, and they offer platitudes because they don't know what else to say. It comforts them, not you. So it can help to come up with back-up answers; I like to make clear that even though I might have another child, I will never have another Soley.

Grieve on your own terms. Don't let anyone pressure you into doing something you're not comfortable with. About six months after Soley died, I had a therapist suggest I get rid of her crib. Just the thought of it made me cry, so I kept the crib and stopped seeing that therapist. It took me nine more months to feel ready to do something about the crib - rather than take it apart, I turned it into a piece of furniture to put her clothes and toys. When it comes to your grief, do what feels right to you, not what looks good to others.

You are not alone. There are many of us out there, and we are your soul sisters. There are meetings and retreats and blogs and Facebook pages and online magazines. When you will need us, we will be here for you. Grieving your baby is the worst thing you'll have to do in your life, but you won't have to do it alone. You can count on us, on our love and our support.

Forever your soul sister,

Chloé, Soley's mom.

https://aboutholland.wordpress.com
http://www.stillmothers.com

"YOU ARE NOT ALONE. THERE ARE MANY OF US OUT THERE, AND WE ARE YOUR SOUL SISTERS."

DEAR LONELY MOTHER,

It's been a little over 2 years and I still recall the way I felt in those first few weeks, and then the first few months, following the loss of my firstborn son. I was numb. I literally felt like I was stuck in a fog. Why me? My Joel was so wanted. He was my world - I had so many plans for him, for his future! We, his parents, loved him! I planned to take him home, not bury him. I picked out his first outfit - but he didn't get to go home in it, he went to the cemetery instead. I felt like my life was frozen in time. The world kept spinning - and after the obligatory expressions of sympathy and concern had ended, I felt I was left alone. Society had moved on. But I wasn't ready. I didn't see how anybody could move on. This was a life-shattering event. My world was dark.

I felt like a mother who didn't even fit in the "loss community" very well for a couple reasons. First, my son wasn't stillborn - it seemed I met many bereaved mothers who had suffered that type of loss. Secondly, I lost him after viability - when he had a medical chance of making it. My son Joel passed away after struggling 2 days in NICU, after being born prematurely. Once I told his father that it felt like a cruel joke to get my hopes up he would survive - only to have him live such a short amount of time. Another way I felt I didn't fit in was because I had no surviving children. I would read a mother post something along the lines of, "My other children are my reason for getting up in the morning." I would get so depressed and angry. They didn't really understand total loss. I had no reason left to get up - I had lost my only child!

As time went on and I continued to struggle with finding some purpose in my life, I would take comfort in the fact that I still had Jay, my son's father and the man I loved. He became my reason to hope. But what I didn't see is that we were grieving differently and drifting apart. Six months after losing our son, to my dismay, we parted ways. My world grew darker as my hope was all but extinguished. I was now utterly and totally alone. Months passed and I just went through the motions - wake up, work, eat, sleep. Somewhere deep inside my fog I began to realize that I needed to accept what happened - and that didn't mean I was saying it was all right that it had. It just meant I was giving myself permission to enjoy life again. It wasn't easy. I felt guilt at times that I was trying to live my life while my son could not. I felt afraid I that he would be forgotten. He already seemed to be remembered less and less with time.

I came to accept that as long as I remembered him, that's what really mattered. I began to find small reasons to smile. I allowed myself to feel something besides sadness. I decided that it was ok to live again. So I began to live - just with a gaping hole in my heart. And you know what? I learned it doesn't go away. You will never be the "old you" ever again - you have permanently changed. And that's ok. Don't expect yourself to get over what happened, because you won't. You don't get over the loss, but you do learn how to live with it. I have learned how to coexist with the pain. And you will too. Give yourself time. I've been there - and I have found a way to cherish Joel's memory while living my life again.

A fellow mommy still missing her boy,

Chrissy

"YOU DON'T GET OVER THE LOSS, BUT YOU DO LEARN HOW TO LIVE WITH IT. I HAVE LEARNED HOW TO COEXIST WITH THE PAIN. AND YOU WILL TOO. GIVE YOURSELF TIME."

DEAR SWEET GRIEVING MOMMA,

I am so very sorry for what you've just lost. Please, before anything else, know that you aren't alone. There are so many people ready and willing to help you as you begin this journey.

I know you're hurting. Probably more than you've ever hurt before. I want you to know though that eventually you'll have good days again. It'll feel weird, and even wrong, but I promise you, it's not. Your sweet child wants you to be happy. I also want you to know that you are allowed to feel whatever you feel. Don't ever let anyone tell you different. Not now and not many years from now.

There is no wrong way to grieve. We all have our own ways. And that's ok.

This will likely be a lifelong journey for you. It has been for me, and many others I know. It's been said that you never truly get over the loss of a child. You adapt to living a new normal. Often, you come to see life differently.

Not everyone will understand. They may say things that will hurt you. Most times it won't be intentional, they won't realize that what they've said has hurt you. Not everyone has lost a child. Then there will be others that you'll hold on to. They will be the ones present with you on your lowest days and your highest days. It may be people from your personal life. It may be people you've yet to meet. All you need to do is look and there will be support, I promise.

My heart breaks for you, as I write this letter. I, like many others, know all too well the heartbreak that is child loss. It has changed my life in ways I didn't think anything could. I'm a different person than who I was before. Please know, we're all here to help you. We all understand.

Sending you so much love, hugs, and warm thoughts.

Thinking of you,

Claire, Leo's momma

www.facebook.com/cblanchard07

"THERE IS NO WRONG WAY TO GRIEVE. WE ALL HAVE OUR OWN WAYS. AND THAT'S OK."

DEAR BEAUTIFUL MAMA,

I am so sorry for the loss of your sweet baby. I know that the pain and grief and numbness and confusion you are feeling now seems unbearable and massive. Babies aren't supposed to die. Yet here you are. Here we both are for I, like you, had to say goodbye far far far too soon.

I know there are no words I can say to fix this or take away your pain. I can't wake you up from this terrible nightmare. I can't fill your empty and aching arms. I can't bring back your precious baby.

But I can say this: You did nothing wrong. You loved your baby and cared for them as fiercely and fully as any mother – and you are a mother, now and always. Nothing and no one can take that away. If anything in this world could overcome death, it would be the deep and powerful love of a parent for their child. You are the fiercest of warrior mamas, carrying love and grief in your very bones through this life without your precious child.

You are not alone. There are many of us who are walking this journey of loss. When you are ready, we are here waiting to wrap you in love. We can't bring them back to you any more than we could have brought our own babies back. We can, however, speak their name with you, remember their lives, honor your beautiful mother love, and stand with you as we hold each other up.

Big Hugs + So Much Love,

Emily
Mama to Grace and Lily, gone too soon

http://emilyrlong.com
http://facebook.com/InvisibleMothers

"YOU DID NOTHING WRONG. YOU LOVED YOUR BABY AND CARED FOR THEM AS FIERCELY AND FULLY AS ANY MOTHER – AND YOU ARE A MOTHER, NOW AND ALWAYS. NOTHING AND NO ONE CAN TAKE THAT AWAY."

DEAR HEARTBROKEN MAMA,

I am writing you to say that I am so sorry. I am so very sorry that you are facing this terrible loss and I wish with all my heart that you were not be reading my letter, that this was not be happening to you. I know how you feel, I understand your pain and your feelings of grief. It is hard to find words that may ease your pain a bit. It is quite impossible.

What I would like to tell you is that even if the physical relationship you have wanted so much is sadly not possible, the relationship between you and your beloved child is a strong and real one. The love you feel, that you have felt for him or her never dies, it will accompany your precious child anywhere. I sincerely believe that this is a very special kind of love. You are a brave and courageous mother, who could not be a better one in any other way.

See, I have always said that children are smarter than us and they know very well who to choose as their mothers, their parents. So, with all that wisdom in their hearts they have picked us. It makes me heartbroken and proud at the same time. I feel privileged to be mother to my sweet little boy. His existence has given me a whole new world. Living this reality without him is not easy, I miss him every second, but if this pain and longing is all I can have with him, I would not trade it for anything.

Listen to your heart and do what you feel like doing. Do whatever makes you feel even just a tiny bit better. There are no rules, no recipes. I wish that you could find the love and gentle care that can protect and comfort you in this lifelong journey of grief. You shouldn't be hard on yourself. Everything you feel, every reaction is just fine. You'll learn and discover ways to express your love, longing and feelings. You'll meet people with similar stories in the most unexpected places. The pain you feel becomes part of who you are, it transforms you. Don't be afraid of it. It takes immensely deep love and a great, courageous soul to carry it.

I wish I could tell you smarter and more comforting things. Unfortunately, I am not capable of doing that. I can only send you all my love, and promise you that if you need me, you can find me and I shall always be there for you.

With all my love and care,

Eva, a mother exactly like you . . .

*"THE LOVE YOU FEEL, THAT YOU HAVE
FELT FOR HIM OR HER NEVER DIES, IT
WILL ACCOMPANY YOUR PRECIOUS CHILD
ANYWHERE. I SINCERELY BELIEVE THAT
THIS IS A VERY SPECIAL KIND OF LOVE.
YOU ARE A BRAVE AND COURAGEOUS
MOTHER, WHO COULD NOT BE A BETTER
ONE IN ANY OTHER WAY."*

DEAR GRIEVING MOMMA,

I wish I had better words to give you, a fellow grieving momma. Your child does matter and will always be with you. I carried my Henry for 21 weeks and 3 days and he lived a few minutes; he is my hero because his life was taken so I could live on and honor him.

Your address book will change but the ones who know you best will be there to pick you up on the days you fall. The best advice I received came in different waves throughout my journey of grief. On the days I was angry, I was told to be kind to myself. The days I was sad, I was told to cry it out. Most of the other days, I was told to just "be" - there is no timeframe of when the hurt will end.

Love,

Heather

Instagram @heatherdockham
Facebook: https://www.facebook.com/heather.dockham

"YOUR ADDRESS BOOK WILL CHANGE BUT THE ONES WHO KNOW YOU BEST WILL BE THERE TO PICK YOU UP ON THE DAYS YOU FALL."

DEAR BEAUTIFUL MOTHER CARRYING TO TERM

I am sorry that you are going through this. My heart breaks for you. I know the pain all too well. I wish there was something that I could do or say to take your pain away or even just lessen it a little. Please know you are not alone, even though it probably feels that way right now. You are a brave, selfless, loving, and strong Mother. You chose life in the midst of darkness and maybe even against the recommendation of others. You chose to enjoy and spend all the time that you have with your precious baby. You refused to allow anyone to take that away from you.

But inside I know you are broken, devastated, confused, and scared. I know you are in so much pain that your heart physically aches. You cry yourself to sleep. You are so angry at times that you just need to scream at the top of your lungs. Nothing else matters to you right now except for your baby. You tell and ask yourself, "This can't be happening to me," "It wasn't supposed to be like this," "Why will my baby die but hers get to live," "What did I do to deserve this," "Why me," "Why babies," and so many more questions and thoughts. I wish I could tell you that you will get answers and understand, but even though you may get some, most will go unanswered. Understand that you are not to blame; you did, and are doing, everything in love for your baby. You will come to feel aged well beyond your years. You will not know what to do or what to say next. There is absolutely nothing wrong with that. Please know that it is ok to break down. It is ok to have all of these emotions. You are living every parent's worst nightmare.

I wish I could tell you that it will be ok, but I can't. I can tell you that you will get through this and you will be forever changed. Take everything second by second, then minute by minute, then hour by hour, then day by day. Allow yourself to grieve and feel all of your emotions. Don't rush yourself, there is no time limit. This grief is part of your "new normal." Don't allow others to rush you or tell you that you are doing it the wrong way. Surround yourself with people who love and support you. Distance yourself from those who don't.

I am sorry those around you are telling you it will all be ok. They share stories of miracles and compare carrying your baby to term with their friend's miscarriage. They tell you that the doctors may be wrong because of some "a friend of a friend" story. I am sorry some of your friends and family are avoiding you like you are contagious. I am sorry for all the horrible comments people are saying to you, "Will you try again," "At least you're young and can have more," "Can you have more," "At least you didn't have much time to get too attached," and so many more. Some mean well but just do not understand. You want this baby. You are attached to this baby. You love this baby.

It does not matter what others think.

Communicate with your husband/partner. Each of you will probably be grieving differently from one another. Spend time together as a family. Go on dates, listen to one another's thoughts and feelings, cry together, and just hold each other.

Take care of you. I know it is hard to even think about that right now, but it is so important. You need emotional, physical, and mental breaks from everything around you. Listen to music, enjoy a cup of tea, read a book, enjoy quiet time alone, take an extra long warm shower or bath, paint your nails, whatever it is that you enjoy.

Oh sweet beautiful Mother, I wish I had the words to truly tell you how sorry I am. It hurts, and while the pain will not be so raw forever, it will always be there. A piece of your heart will always be missing. Know that you are not betraying your precious baby by living your life and moving forward, because you will always have their memory and the love you have for them in your heart.

I have you my prayers and thoughts, Matthew 5:4.

You are a beautiful Mother.

Love Always,

Heather

"I WISH I COULD TELL YOU THAT IT WILL BE OK, BUT I CAN'T. I CAN TELL YOU THAT YOU WILL GET THROUGH THIS AND YOU WILL BE FOREVER CHANGED. TAKE EVERYTHING SECOND BY SECOND, THEN MINUTE BY MINUTE, THEN HOUR BY HOUR, THEN DAY BY DAY."

DEAR BEREAVED MOM,

I've written to you to tell you how sorry I am that we are meeting, that we have joined this "club." I don't know where you may be in your journey in grieving for your child. As I sit here 7 1/2 months after losing my daughter, I feel that what I would have wanted to hear those first few days is the same as I would like to hear now. I wanted to know that it was okay to feel devastated. I still want to know that it is okay to be devastated. I wanted to hear that no matter how old my baby girl was when she died, she died. I did not "mis"carry her. I did not lose a pregnancy. My daughter died. And her life, no matter how short, mattered. And your child's life mattered too.

I have pondered recently whether or not peace and pain can coexist. As I write this tonight, I believe, in fact, that is what grief is. I've come to this place of peace with a pain so deep that it takes my breath away at moments. I've found peace in holding on to the love that filled my heart the moment that I saw those two blue lines. I've found peace in searching for signs from Heaven of my baby girl. I've found peace in my faith that she is with God.

As I imagine a newly bereaved mommy reading this, I realize how hard it may be to imagine a day or space with peace. The pain is so overwhelming that there seems no hope of peace. I won't tell you that the pain goes away. I, myself, don't want to lose the pain as it feels like losing the pain would mean losing the existence of my daughter in my life. She is and always will be in my heart and soul. Until I lost her, the notion of anything being a part of my heart and soul just seemed like a saying. I never knew such love could fill my being as the love I've come to know for my daughter.

The fact that you may be reading this book means that you have already found this community of other bereaved mommies. I want you to know that this community has been an amazing source of support and strength for me. I would never have managed through my journey without hearing the words of validation, love, courage, and encouragement from these other mommies. I pray your journey continues to connect you with other loving mommies. I pray that you find peace with the pain. I pray that you find ways to keep your baby's memory alive in your life. And I pray for you to find love and support here and in your own community.

Love and light,

Jenifer

https://jeniferruby.wordpress.com

*"I WANTED TO HEAR THAT NO MATTER
HOW OLD MY BABY GIRL WAS WHEN SHE
DIED, SHE DIED. I DID NOT "MIS"CARRY
HER. I DID NOT LOSE A PREGNANCY. MY
DAUGHTER DIED. AND HER LIFE, NO
MATTER HOW SHORT, MATTERED. AND
YOUR CHILD'S LIFE MATTERED TOO."*

DEAR MOMMA,

I am so very sorry for the loss of your precious baby. I am holding you so very close in this broken heart of mine. I will say the name of your sweet child with you. Right now, that is the only strength I know for sure, and these days I don't know much. I do know the power of saying your baby's name out loud for the world to hear. I will say it clearly and with the most stubborn strength I have left in me. Even if it's just in our own little corners.

I will share my daughter's name with you too. Leona Grace.

You will hear and feel so many things. Some will take your breath away and others will knock you off your feet. Friends may become strangers, and strangers will become friends. These new friends will speak to your heart, lift up your soul and hold you close. You are never alone.

I wish so much for you, my friend. Just as I do for my heart. For you, I have space for wishes too.

I wish for you to be surrounded in care and comfort, whatever that may be. I wish you a large pillow or a weighted bear when the tears sting with pain. I wish you a warm cup of tea when the quiet weeping sets in. I wish you a witness when the outrage burns to be heard. I wish you a listening ear from a compassionate soul. I wish you eyes that will cry *with* you. I wish you a hand to soothe or a hug to hold you. I wish you words that are healing and filled with love, words that your heart will remember most amid the noise.

When you are ready for the outside world, I am still wishing these things for you. I wish you a neighbor who will smile when you need it or give you simple conversation. I wish you the most beautiful sunshine when you want to feel warmth. I wish you days in bed, listening to the rain when you want to feel Nature mourn *with* you. I wish you moments of needed silence and solace. I wish you moments of lightness. I wish you the kind of support that you need, near and far.

Mostly, I wish you have just one person in your life, even if it's just you, who will speak your baby's name every day. I wish you have the space to tell your story and your baby's story. I wish that your heart will never let go of this fact - You are a Mother.

If you ever needed any of that reflected back to you, here in these pages, we are all with you. Heart to heart, hand in hand.

I wish you love, Momma.

Kimberly Roth

Mommy to Leona Grace, born August 26, 2015
mommamighty.wordpress.com

"I WISH YOU HAVE JUST ONE PERSON IN YOUR LIFE, EVEN IF IT'S JUST YOU, WHO WILL SPEAK YOUR BABY'S NAME EVERY DAY. I WISH YOU HAVE THE SPACE TO TELL YOUR STORY AND YOUR BABY'S STORY. I WISH THAT YOUR HEART WILL NEVER LET GO OF THIS FACT - YOU ARE A MOTHER."

DEAR MAMA,

I see your hurting heart and I wish I could be there with you. I'd bring you a nice warm drink (chai, hot chocolate, tea, it's your pick), perhaps some marshmallows too, and just sit with you. I wouldn't say much because I know there's not much to say. Your precious baby has died and you are wondering how to go on. I've asked myself so many times in the months and years since Ariella was stillborn. That gut-wrenching pain you feel? The shattered heart that you aren't sure will ever mend? I felt it too. I still do. You are not alone. But if you are like me, you probably do feel alone. After all, no one had the same relationship with your child as you. No one loved them like you and no one grieves like you. A mother's love is like no other, so while others do love and grieve for your child, your broken heart is unique.

As we sip our hot chocolates together (probably wearing our pajamas because everyone knows they are the most comfortable thing), there is one thing I will say. *You will get through this.* Others will expect you to "get over" your loss but that is impossible. We grieve because we love and we cannot and will not "get over" our love for our babies. But I promise you that you will get through. "How?" you may ask.

When Ariella died that was my number one question; I asked every bereaved mother that I knew. I simply could not imagine how I could get up each day, knowing that the gaping hole in my heart would be there every day. The pain I felt at her death was amplified whenever I thought about the fact that it wasn't a bad dream and that this was my new reality. I asked the question so many times and I got the same answer no matter who I asked: the way to get through isn't one year, one month or even one day at a time. We get through by taking things one moment at a time.

When the pain strikes, breathe.

When guilt attacks because you dared to laugh, breathe.

And one day, when you find yourself experiencing true joy again, breathe.

Soak it in.

You can do this, sweet mama. I, along with a whole community of mamas, am cheering you on as you tackle life without your child. You are not alone.

With love,

Larissa

www.loveisdeeperstill.blogspot.com
www.facebook.com/loveisdeeperstill

"THE WAY TO GET THROUGH ISN'T ONE YEAR, ONE MONTH OR EVEN ONE DAY AT A TIME. WE GET THROUGH BY TAKING THINGS ONE MOMENT AT A TIME."

DEAR HURTING MOM

I am so very sorry you are with us on this journey. The pain, darkness, and confusion that come with it cannot be put into words. Only those of us who are on this same path can understand what you are dealing with.

There are two things I feel in my heart that I want you to know.

First, you are not alone. Not only do you have us by your side, but you have the One who can help you navigate through these suffocating waters. Yes, I know you are probably angry with Him right now, because He did not stop your child from leaving this earth. He did not stop mine either.

We all ask "Why?" Why me? Why my child? If He were to give us an answer, it wouldn't be good enough though, in our intense pain. And to be honest, if I could rub a magic lamp and make God do what I wanted Him to do, He would no longer be big enough to be God.

For me, when I moved from the question "why" to the question "how", it started the process of climbing out of the pit of blackness. "How am I going to live through this to be a mom to my other children?" "How can I honor my daughter with life, instead of with my own emotional death?"

I will never be the same, and I still miss her and shed tears, but the pain is not a stabbing-can't-function kind of pain any more.

The second thing is that you will need to choose to forgive, so you don't become an angry, bitter person for the rest of your life. As parents who have lost a child, there are so many people we need to forgive:

- God, for not saving our child
- Anyone who had anything even remotely to do with how or why he or she died
- Ourselves, for not being able to stop it somehow
- Our child for dying and leaving us

I encourage you to go through each of these, and tell each one out loud you forgive them (including yourself). Forgiveness is not based on how we feel. It is based on a choice we make to not be emotionally disabled by our anger and bitterness. It isn't freeing them, it is freeing *you*! Do it as often as you need to, for however long it takes to actually get free of your blame and anger.

There is hope. If you can't see it or feel it right now, we are here to hold on to it for you, until you can grab hold of it for yourself.

You have my hugs, my heart, and my prayers.

Laura Diehl

Website for GPS Hope (Grieving Parents Sharing Hope)
www.gpshope.org
Facebook page - GPS Hope: Grieving Parents Sharing Hope

"THERE IS HOPE. IF YOU CAN'T SEE IT OR FEEL IT RIGHT NOW, WE ARE HERE TO HOLD ON TO IT FOR YOU, UNTIL YOU CAN GRAB HOLD OF IT FOR YOURSELF."

DEAR GRIEVING MOTHER,

Yesterday, you were a version of yourself that will never be again. It's ok to let go of that person and to embrace the unknown that lies before you. It's ok to be scared, but I know you can do this.

The hardest part is first feel everything. All of the horrible and painful. Scream it, talk it, write it, punch a pillow - just feel it and say it. Get it out. Be raw and angry. Do not put a brave face on. Tell your truth. Let yourself be vulnerable. Genuinely grieve. There's no right way, there's no timetable. Follow what your body/mind/soul tells you.

For a while, it will feel like you are a complete stranger - to those around you and to yourself. You will need to re learn how to become comfortable in your own skin again and there will be growing pains. Parts of the old you will come back and blend in with the new. Roll with it.

Then comes some awkward parts - there will be lots of reminders of the memories you wish you could be making. If you look a little harder, you'll see the opportunities to make other beautiful ones you never dreamed possible and wouldn't have seen otherwise. Don't give up on yourself, you've survived a big chunk of this and will thrive again. Honour your babies by living on so their memory does too.

Start making new memories when you are ready - from something as small as changing one or two things in your daily routine (such as taking a different route into town or shop at a different grocery store) to the bigger things (what you do for a living, how you spend your off time, making new traditions for yourself that hold meaning in the world as it now is for you).

Then this will happen - you will experience joy again and you may feel guilty for it. Taking joy in anything again without your beloved child here with you often feels wrong. I want you to know that it is not your lot in life to remain here suffering - you are not being punished, you have done nothing wrong. Feel that joy - you have earned it and you deserve it.

There is a place for you, and the love for your child, to live on in this world. You are a rarity - the exception to the rule. Don't deny yourself the motherly things you would've done for your child. Love and care for everyone (including yourself) with every ounce of your being the way you would your baby. Be a Mom - wear that badge with honour - for you are nothing less. You are however also so much more now - you are the mother of all mothers.

Love,

Lindsay

"TELL YOUR TRUTH. LET YOURSELF BE VULNERABLE. GENUINELY GRIEVE. THERE'S NO RIGHT WAY, THERE'S NO TIMETABLE. FOLLOW WHAT YOUR BODY/ MIND/SOUL TELLS YOU."

TO THE BEAUTIFUL AND BROKEN MAMA ON THE MORNING AFTER YOUR HEART WAS TORN FROM YOUR SOUL,

I can tell you that today, you will wake up, even if you don't want to. The cruel joke of the world is that you are still here and your child is not, on this first day of life now split into the forever proverbial "before" and "after" your child died.

You will rise, just like the sun, if you want to or not but mostly because you have no other choice. You may awake alone in your own bed or your child's empty one, where you passed out the night before in a puddle of disbelieving tears. Or maybe you wake in a hospital bed like I did, cradled in the hands of your loving husband who rouses you with his gentle hand softly stroking your cheek.

For less than a moment you will forget, be disorientated, and think that all is right in the world and life was still like the "before," before this horrible curse was bestowed on you. But then, oh my blessed and heartbroken friend, oh how I wish this part of the day wouldn't happen, but it will because, as you soon and so ruthlessly will learn, reality always wins and it will set in. In about another millisecond, your body will heave with agony and disbelief when you remember that today is the first day of the life in the "after" your child died.

When this realization washes over your being, you might need to catch your breath because, for what will feel like an eternity, you won't be able to breathe. How could you any longer, part of your soul has been extinguished. It's as if a part of your own body is missing, your child, gone.

All I can tell you, beautifully broken mama, is that I too have had this morning. I too struggled to find air to breathe, words to speak that weren't smothered in tears, and ground to stand on that wasn't quick sand beneath my feet. I too know the excruciating pain that comes with losing a child. And yes, the emotional pain of it all hurts so much more than any physical pain could. Chop off my arm, take my leg, and gouge out my eyes. Any of that, all of that, would have been easier to bear than losing my sweet baby. Losing a child is torture to the soul.

All I can tell you, beautiful and broken mama, is I too have been beaten and battered in this way. I want to tell you that it gets easier, that it won't hurt as much as it does today, on day one of the "after" as much as it will on day 847. I so much want to say those words to you, but that would be lying and it would invalidate your love, longing, and your grief.

What I can tell you is it's different today, on day 847 of the "after" than it is on day one. Just as it will be different tomorrow on day two, five, and thirty.

What I can tell you is that you will always love and miss your child and that you will never forget them or the joy and love they brought to your life no matter how painful it is to remember.

What I can tell you is that you will carry on. You will survive and there will even be days in the "after" where you smile and laugh again. Sometimes as with just as full of a lightness and joy as in the days of "before".

I know it's hard to believe now. I know this is the worst thing life will ever throw at you.

I know.

And I know you can survive...

because I have survived too.

And from my day 847 of the "after," I'm sorry. I'm crying for you as I write this, I'm crying for the me on day one because I know it is so hard. But here on day 847 I am okay. And most importantly I want you know that I am with you and so are all the other bereaved mothers who have been through day one. I am here as a testament that you will make it through this. You will survive. And I am sending you love and light from my 847th day to you on your day one.

Sincerely,

Lindsey M. Henke

- A broken and still beautiful bereaved mama

Pregnancy After Loss Support: https://pregnancyafterlosssupport.com/

*"WHAT I CAN TELL YOU IS THAT YOU WILL
CARRY ON. YOU WILL SURVIVE AND THERE
WILL EVEN BE DAYS IN THE "AFTER"
WHERE YOU SMILE AND LAUGH AGAIN."*

DEAR MOMMA,

I can't tell you how many times I've written, and re-written, this letter to you. I lost count several drafts ago. I keep trying to find the perfect words for you. In my mind, I know the perfect words don't exist. But my heart wants me to keep searching. I keep questioning myself and seconding guessing everything I want to tell you. As loss mothers, that's what we tend to do, right? We question ourselves and worry we are making the wrong decisions. We always go back to the "what-ifs."

I'm just going to let my heart speak, and for once, not question anything. My heart is wide open to you. My heart breaks for you and your beloved child. I wish, with everything inside me, that you were blissfully unaware of what it means to be a loss mother. I wish you didn't know the intense feelings of anger, sorrow, loneliness, and confusion that come with child loss. Those feelings are so awful, I would never wish them on anyone. I wish I could take away your pain and carry it for you. As a bereaved mother, you will carry your grief with you for the rest of your life. Over time, you grief may feel like less of a burden. It will change, but it will always be there. It will remain with you because you love your child so deeply.

Of all the things I've learned since my daughter passed away, there are two simple words that help me get through most days – *it's okay*. It's okay to scream and cry. It's okay to question everything you've ever thought to be true. It's okay to feel like a different person. You *are* a different person. You will never be the *old* you again. It's okay to smile and laugh again. It's okay to look for happiness again. It's okay to feel tired. It's okay to walk away from people who aren't supportive. It's okay to hide from the world when you need to. It's okay to embrace your sorrow and happiness, together and separately.

It's okay.

Whatever you are feeling, at any given moment, is valid. You didn't ask for this. You aren't being punished for anything. None of this is your fault. You have a right to grieve, and heal, in your own way. The one thing that will <u>never</u> be okay is the harsh, unfair, and undeserved reality of your status as a bereaved mother. You've suffered one of the most significant losses in life. *That* will never be okay. I am so sorry this tragedy cannot be undone. I wish there was a re-do button for all loss mothers – not so we had to go through the heartache all over again – so we could spend just one more moment with our children.

Please always remember that you are not alone. There are many of us who are walking along the same path. We're here for you.

Lastly, but certainly most important of all, please always remember that no matter what you do, or how you feel, the bond you have with your child will never be broken. The love you share will live on forever. Don't ever be afraid to speak your child's name. Your precious child matters and deserves to be remembered.

Sweet momma, you are beautiful, courageous, and resilient. Above all else, you are a mother. Nothing will ever change that.

Love,

Elliot's Momma
Lori Davis

Blog - www.walkingwithelliot.com

"PLEASE ALWAYS REMEMBER THAT YOU ARE NOT ALONE. THERE ARE MANY OF US WHO ARE WALKING ALONG THE SAME PATH. WE'RE HERE FOR YOU."

DEAR MAMA,

It's weird to hear that, isn't it?
You know you are a Mama.

And yet...

Your baby is gone.

There is no heartbeat anymore.

The doctors don't know what to tell you.

The waiting car seat will forever be empty.

I know.
I know.

That was the worst for me—the minute that reality actually
set in.

I got into my car, barely able to stand after a day of labor and
an unexpected surgery in which I nearly died.
I looked into the backseat, and there it was.

My first-born's car seat.

Empty, looming and taunting.

He was perfectly healthy. A week overdue.
First world babies don't die because of labor complications.

But they do.

Mine did.

This pain you feel—the aching that you didn't even know could possibly exist?

Don't let anyone tell you not to feel it.

It's the deepest, darkest and most horrific pain you will ever feel. Ever. And you will wish with all your might you didn't have to feel it. I so wish you didn't have to.

People will tell you not to feel it.
Some will do so because they want to protect you, protect your heart and your soul.

Others will tell you not to feel it because it makes them uncomfortable.

Others still will tell you not to feel it because they don't have the slightest bit of reference for how life-changing this is, and that lack of perspective is a gift for them but a curse for you.

Ignore them all.

Feel *whatever you need* to feel to survive.

Breathing will be laborious.

Opening your eyes every morning will be like sticking a knife in your heart, and often bring you to your knees wishing you could just close your eyes again and keep them closed forever.

And you will need to know that *this is normal.*
You've lost a most precious part of yourself, and that metamorphosis is a painful one.

That change, though…those heavy chains that feel like anchors every.single.day?
I need you to know that they change too.

They get lighter, and even though it sounds ridiculous to say, more bearable.
One day, you'll even feel like they're not even heavy at all.
They'll become a part of you too—reminding you that it wasn't all a dream, and that you did, indeed, suffer the most traumatic loss imaginable and *survived.*

In fact, some days, the anchors will not even feel like anchors, but beacons, even…guiding you to places you'd never go and into things you'd never do if you didn't have them as your experience guides.

They're always there—but you get to choose how you wear them. That you didn't choose them makes no difference…no one ever does or would, and so, the choice comes in how we carry them.

My heart is breaking for you as you read this. I remember the days I would read things and think, "There is no way this person loved her child as much as I loved mine. She could NEVER say this if she did. *I will never escape this pain.*"

I get it, friend. I do.

But I have to tell you, because I was so desperate to know it then myself…

You can and will breathe again.
You can and will smile again.
You can and will laugh again.
You can and will claim happiness again, even if a different one that you never predicted.

And most importantly, you will *always, always* be his or her Mama, and there is a sisterhood of mothers who will stand with you and walk with you every step of the way, until you find the strength to do so on your own.

You are not alone.

Lori

www.stillstandingmag.com
http://www.loridoesmd.blogspot.com/

"FEEL WHATEVER YOU NEED TO FEEL TO SURVIVE."

DEAR MOMMA,

Your world has just fallen part. Every inch of you is broken. Your heart, torn into a million little pieces, is still somehow beating. Time has stopped for you, but yet all around you, the world keeps on spinning. Nothing makes sense, because something so senseless has occurred. What should have been the most exciting moment of your life is now the line that divides the before and after.

You don't think you're going to survive. You think your life is over. Yes, you are living, but you are not alive. You are angry because, after all, life has dealt you with an unfair hand. You are now forced to learn a lesson that you didn't want to learn. The universe, it feels, has somehow marked you for a punishment you don't deserve.

There is no anguish in the world that can match a grieving mother, and you, my dear momma, you now know it so well.

Your life may feel like it's over, but it's not.

You are at the halfway mark.

The halfway point that marks the before and after. This after is a new world. A new world in which you will learn to live again. To smile again. To be part of the living.

One day you will be able to go out into the world and learn

to talk and act like the old you again. You will catch glimpses of her in the mirror, the same look but the light in the eyes will always be different.

You are now in the after.

This is a different world now and you will find yourself with bouts of fear as the world moves on without your precious child. But I assure you, your child is always with you. You will occasionally have fear that you will forget your child, but I promise you that your love will always be a testament to their existence. When you love someone so deeply, nothing can shake that bond.

The after is where you will learn how powerful love really is, how something once broken can be put back into place and be turned into something more powerful and beautiful.

It's not over. You are at the halfway mark.

Love,

Malka

"YOU WILL OCCASIONALLY HAVE FEAR THAT YOU WILL FORGET YOUR CHILD, BUT I PROMISE YOU THAT YOUR LOVE WILL ALWAYS BE A TESTAMENT TO THEIR EXISTENCE. WHEN YOU LOVE SOMEONE SO DEEPLY, NOTHING CAN SHAKE THAT BOND."

DEAR MOTHER OF A CHILD GONE TOO SOON,

You are not alone.

These are the most important words I could share with you. These simple words are what I desperately needed to hear— apart from, "Your son is ok! He's still alive!"—in the days after my baby died, and even now, more than two years after.

I know these are probably not the words you will hear from your family and friends. You'll likely hear so many unhelpful things, though: "Maybe it just wasn't meant to be," or "There must be some reason we can't understand," or, one of the worst and most despised from my experience, "You have to be lucky in life." Well, I guess I'm very "unlucky" then, even more so my son. But we're not the only ones. So unfairly and so gut-wrenchingly, we're not the only ones, as much as family and friends—pretty much all of society—try to sweep that ugly fact under the rug.

No, you're far from alone, although maybe you, like me, have felt that way after the death of your child. The truth is, you and your child were just as worthy of life—a good, happy, long life—as anyone with a beating heart who occupies space on this Earth. You and your child weren't singled out because you were any less deserving than those who are privileged to be living right now, those given the chance at a childhood, adulthood, a family of their own. What everyone else takes for granted. You're not any less than the mothers who've been gifted with children who will live hours, months, years more than your child did. All the "lucky" mothers who will never have to hear those final, devastating words of loss, or witness and bear their child's departure.

You are not alone. Even if it feels that way when friends and family talk about their living children and never mention yours who died, but whose existence remains just as valid (and your love as a mother just as fierce). Even when people avoid talking to you altogether, as if you've scattered eggshells all around you, as if the slight cracking of your voice as you speak about your child might shatter their sense of security, their buffer from pain. Even if there is radio silence on your child's birthday, due date or "angelversary," you are not alone.

You are not alone, even though our stories are unique, and our children irreplaceable individuals, each an unmatched contribution to this world. Even if the rest of society dismisses your unique story, your unique child, your unique family, your unique pain, you are not alone. I acknowledge you. I acknowledge your tragedy, your grief. I acknowledge your precious child. You and your child are not alone.

My heart goes out to you,

Maria LoPiccolo

Mother of Bruce Gasca LoPiccolo (9-20-13 – 9-23-13)

"*I ACKNOWLEDGE YOU. I ACKNOWLEDGE YOUR TRAGEDY, YOUR GRIEF. I ACKNOWLEDGE YOUR PRECIOUS CHILD. YOU AND YOUR CHILD ARE NOT ALONE.*"

DEAR TWINLESS TWIN MOMMA,

I know. I know how broken you are. I know you see two when there is only one. I know you can't understand how there is only one of your twins left.

I know because I still don't understand how only one of mine is left.

It doesn't make sense and perhaps, for both of us, it never will. Navigating this new world as a twinless twin momma is hard. And confusing. There is joy one minute, and devastation the next. Your world will never be balanced.

But there is peace. Not the type of peace that balances and is neatly tied up in a box, but peace nonetheless.

It will take time. And tears. Lots of tears, filled with sorrow, heartache, and dreams that became beyond your reach when your baby died. The questioning will never end and your heart won't ever be healed this side of Heaven.

The peace will find you before you know it does. One day you'll look up and realize that you don't see two anymore. You won't always be looking for your baby's other half. And you'll be able to marvel in your surviving twin's accomplishments without tears falling. You will feel able to parent. Maybe for the first time if your twins were your first babies, or maybe once again if you have older children.

You will eventually feel able to pick yourself up off the ground, put your big girl shoes on and figure out how to live.

But today, you only need to survive. Maybe for the next minute, maybe for the next hour – just survive. Know that you are not alone. It's a special type of grief when you lose one of your twins. It's happy and sad, celebration and devastation, its surviving with your heart being pulled in two directions every minute: life and death.

Maybe you had both for a little bit, or maybe you delivered one alive and one sleeping. I hope you got to hold them both at the same time - even just once. I hope you have pictures of them together.

I hope you know their bond will never die. I know because I have seen it in my own surviving twin.

I hope you know your bond with your baby will never die. I know because mine has not.

I know. And I'm so, so sorry that you have found this awful club.

Love,

Will and MJ's Momma
Will, Twin A - Surviving and
Thriving Age 6
MJ, Twin B - Forever 35 Days

"I HOPE YOU KNOW YOUR BOND WITH YOUR BABY WILL NEVER DIE. I KNOW BECAUSE MINE HAS NOT."

DEAR SISTER,

When I was 27 weeks pregnant with my first child and the doctors told me my baby would likely not survive, I looked up tearfully at my midwife and asked, "What do I say when people ask how many kids do I have?" She whispered, "I don't know," as empathetically as possible. "How do I do this?" I asked, receiving no real answer.

Now two years after my daughter's birth and her death shortly after, I am not sure I have the answer. How do you do this? I don't know. I think you simply just do it. Somehow. Someway. You survive.

After I lost her, I remember reading the words of fellow bereaved parents two years out, who had said it gets better. At the time those words didn't comfort me. I didn't want the hurt to go away because I thought it meant leaving behind my daughter. But I also didn't want to hurt anymore. I realize now that I just wanted my daughter back. Now I am that person two years out and I struggle to find words that will bring you some sort of comfort.

So all I can do is tell you how I found my answer to that first question that brought me so much distress, "How many kids do you have?" Every time someone asked, I experimented with different responses. I can see now, my responses and reactions evolved as my grief did.

None.
None living.
I had a daughter.
I had a daughter but she died after birth.
I had a daughter but she died last year.

I learned that I had to find the words that made me feel the best. Many women change what they say depending on who they are talking to - at times protecting the memories of their children when talking to strangers and being more open with people who they will interact with again. Some women change the subject or ignore the question. It's not the response that matters, but how the response makes you feel. You will find what works. There is no one way to do it.

Test it out. Think of a few options of how you might respond. Try each out in different interactions and see how you feel. I learned that when people start closing down after learning of my daughter's death, it helped to say "Thank you. Thank you for asking. I like talking about her," which puts them at ease and is truth to me. When I don't want to talk about her, I simply change the subject after I hear the requisite, "I'm sorry."

In the beginning it was hard. My heart raced; my palms

sweated. I stumbled over the words. Now my response flows easily, though I still feel a flush when asked the question. Just like my grief - at first it was hard, very physical pain. With time and practice I learned to incorporate my grief into my daily life. You will too. Just like me, you will survive.

Wishing you strength,

Mabel's Mom
Meghan Constantino

www.expectingthunexpectedblog.wordpress.com

"WITH TIME AND PRACTICE I LEARNED TO INCORPORATE MY GRIEF INTO MY DAILY LIFE. YOU WILL TOO. JUST LIKE ME, YOU WILL SURVIVE."

DEAR LOSS MOM,

I am so sorry that you are reading this. Losing a child is a devastating loss. There is no heartbreak greater than having to say goodbye to your precious and much loved child.

Remember to be gentle with yourself. Your world has been turned upside down and ripped apart. The loss, pain and trauma you are experiencing is so great, please be kind to yourself. This journey is one of the most difficult you can take as a mother. Be gentle with yourself as you navigate it. If all you can do today is breathe, that is enough. Just breathe.

There are so many emotions washing over you, it can feel like you are drowning. The pain, the numbness, the heartbreak, the anger, the sadness, the loneliness. . .It can feel as though it is too much, but just keep breathing. Even during the times when you feel completely broken, just keep breathing. You will survive this, even when it feels impossible.

Please believe that it won't always hurt so much. It seems impossible to believe that you could feel anything other than broken and sad, that you will ever laugh again, feel joy or be at peace. But hold on to the hope that it is true, because it is. One day you will feel almost whole again, even if a piece of your heart will forever be missing. Grief, especially the grief of losing a child, takes much time and effort to work through.

But things will get better, you won't always feel so broken.

Know that you aren't alone. There is a whole tribe of loss mothers who have been where you are. Reach out to them, hold on to them. When you lose a child, the emotions are so intense, it can feel like you're losing your mind. Hearing others' stories and knowing they've been where you are is reassuring that you aren't alone. You are deep within your grief and it is hard to find your way on your own. Find people who will listen and be there for you without judgment or trying to fix it. It could be a friend, a family member, a counselor, another loss mom.

Losing a child will change you forever. Eventually you will find your new normal. Give yourself time and space to find this new normal. Some things that helped me after my son died were:

- Trying to let go of asking "Why?" Sometimes there just aren't any answers, no matter how much we want them. My search to find the answer to "Why my sweet baby had to die?" made me feel frantic and helpless. Once I was able to let go of needing to know why, I felt calmer and made room in my heart for acceptance to begin.

- Spending time every day doing something that brings

peace to your raw and broken heart. For me, it was getting outside and walking my dog. Even when I didn't want to and had to force myself, I walked every day and it was very healing. Grief can be such a deep pit. Forcing yourself out of that pit, even for a few minutes, is so important for your heart and mind.

-   Creating traditions to celebrate and include your child. We fill my son's stocking with Christmas messages, light a candle for him on special days, throw feathers in the wind on his birthday, include his lion stuffed toy in family photos, and teach our two younger children about him. These traditions bring me peace knowing he will always be included as part of our family. Your sweet child will never be forgotten. They will be woven into every day of your life. Your child will be remembered, loved and cherished.

Stay strong Mama. With your precious child forever in your heart, you will survive the impossible.

With loving and gentle thoughts,

Melissa
Angel Mama to Aiden

"THIS JOURNEY IS ONE OF THE MOST DIFFICULT YOU CAN TAKE AS A MOTHER. BE GENTLE WITH YOURSELF AS YOU NAVIGATE IT. IF ALL YOU CAN DO TODAY IS BREATHE, THAT IS ENOUGH. JUST BREATHE."

HI MOMMA,

I am so sorry you are finding yourself reading this book. My heart goes out to you. I don't know your situation or where you are with your grief or how long you've been on this journey, but I do know that you are not alone. Let me say that again...You Are Not Alone. Unfortunately loss moms have come before you and loss moms will come after you. I wish I had known this when I lost my first son, Joshua. I felt alone. I felt like no one understood the pain I felt so deep in my heart. If you remember nothing else I mention, please always remember that.

I wish I could tell you the pain will go away, but it won't. It will always be there. Birthdays, holidays and anniversaries will be hard. Sometimes, just because it is Monday, it will be hard. But, you will learn your "new normal." Living your life without your child will never get easier, but you will smile again. Not that fake smile you've been giving people, but a real genuine smile. You'll laugh again too. You may feel guilty when you do, but please try not to.

Don't be afraid to reach out or seek professional help if you feel you need it. If you don't have other living children, don't let anyone tell you that you aren't a mom. You absolutely are. Don't be afraid to speak your child's name. Don't worry about what others may think if your baby passed away early in pregnancy and you decide to name your baby. My second child left us at nine weeks and his name is Matthew.

Try to remember that your family and friends do have good intentions, but sometimes they may say things they think are helpful, but it really aren't and sometimes what they say may make you mad. That is normal. Speaking of normal. . .you might not like pregnant women for awhile or you may find yourself browsing the baby section in a store imagining what could have been. You may have phantom baby kicks or movement. This is all totally normal. Don't let anyone tell you any different.

Please remember to take time for you if you need to. Remember your significant other is hurting also. You both need one another now more than ever. Lean on each other. They will try to be strong for you, but let them know it is okay to break down.

If you believe in God or someone/something else, you may question that higher power. This may weaken or strengthen the faith you have for said higher power. I suggest you speak to someone that is familiar with your beliefs and let them help you if you find yourself questioning things.

If you ever need an ear or two, please know that I am here for you and so are so many others.

With love,

Michele Zahniser

Angel Mommy of Joshua - 5/20/09 & Matthew - 1/2/11

"LIVING YOUR LIFE WITHOUT YOUR CHILD WILL NEVER GET EASIER, BUT YOU WILL SMILE AGAIN. NOT THAT FAKE SMILE YOU'VE BEEN GIVING PEOPLE, BUT A REAL GENUINE SMILE. YOU'LL LAUGH AGAIN TOO."

DEAR NEW GRIEVING MOTHER,

First, I want to say that I am so sorry you have joined me as a grieving mother. No mother should ever have to lose a child and we have survived the unthinkable. I hope that you are able to find support and that you will not feel alone through this journey that began when you lost your precious child. The grief following your loss will not stay with you forever, you will eventually begin to feel happy again, there is a light at the end of the tunnel (although sometimes hard to find!)

I've been on the receiving end of bad news, hearing the words "there is no heartbeat." I've labored for countless hours to give birth to a baby that I know has already passed. I've woken up in an ICU bed, completely alone and scared to my core. I'm still here today. I made it through each and every one of those moments. I lived life in a fog for quite some time but I fought hard to keep pushing forward and have found happiness once again.

You too, will someday be able to fondly remember your child and the happy moments that you shared. When you're feeling sad, lonely or afraid of what should come next for your life, reach out and seek support. My hardest days were also my loneliest days. There won't ever be anything that can replace your child or the time you've lost with them but there are angel parents throughout the world that understand all too well what you are going through.

You're in my thoughts. Be strong, you've got this mama!

Natalie Welanetz

http://healinggracebirthsupport.com/
https://www.facebook.com/hgracedoulas

"YOU TOO, WILL SOMEDAY BE ABLE TO FONDLY REMEMBER YOUR CHILD AND THE HAPPY MOMENTS THAT YOU SHARED."

DEAR BEAUTIFUL MOTHER,

My heart is with you.

I have walked this path you're now walking. I've hurt these hurts. I've screamed these screams. I've questioned these unanswerable questions. I've known the love that seeps from your every pore, and the pain that seems to have no end. I've felt the confusion and anguish swirling around your head and the gaping hole in your heart.

You are not alone.

I know what it is to feel like you're dead, but unable to die. I know what it means to want to burst from the madness. I know what it feels like to be angry from the depths of your soul. To be blindsided by the lack of support from people you thought would always be there. To drive yourself crazy wondering why and how this happened. To question everything you've ever believed in. To feel completely broken. To feel a longing for your child that's so strong you can hardly believe it. To miss your sweet little one with every cell in your body. To feel astounded this is actually your life.

You're not doing it wrong.

I know how it feels to think of every single reason why this could be your fault, even though it's impossible that you actually caused it. I know what it means to feel like an absolute failure as a woman. To hate your body. To burn with jealousy at the undeserving mothers whose child lived. To want to crawl in a hole forever when your friends and family announce they are expecting. To hate everyone and everything.

You're not a bad person. You're a mother living without her baby.

I want you to know that grief changes you; just like the love you have for your child changed you. You will never be the same again. Don't let anyone push you to "get back to normal." There's no such thing as back to normal after devastating loss like this. But please hold on, I promise you can do this. Even if it's just one breath to the next - and it's perfectly okay if that's all you do sometimes - just hold on.

You will survive.

As you learn to live without your sweet baby - and believe me, I know that the last thing you want to do - you'll see how the love you hold in your heart will continue growing with each passing day. You'll learn how to hold your child in your heart while also relearning to live. The pain will change with a lot of work, and in a lot of time, but the love will never go away. You will have horrible days, and bad days, and numb days, and okay days. After some time, you'll even have good days. And always, your child will remain safely tucked in your heart.

Be gentle with yourself.

Grief is as unique as your child, and there is no right or wrong way to grieve. Follow your heart. Trust your instincts. Let go of the expectations of others. Allow the love for your child to guide you towards healing. When it hurts the most, remember this: grief is made of love. You hurt intensely because you love deeply. And that makes you the best mother your baby could have.

With Samuel in my heart,

RaeAnne

www.stillmothers.com
https://www.facebook.com/AllThatLoveCanDo/

"GRIEF IS AS UNIQUE AS YOUR CHILD, AND THERE IS NO RIGHT OR WRONG WAY TO GRIEVE. FOLLOW YOUR HEART. TRUST YOUR INSTINCTS. LET GO OF THE EXPECTATIONS OF OTHERS. ALLOW THE LOVE FOR YOUR CHILD TO GUIDE YOU TOWARDS HEALING."

DEAR LOSS MOTHER,

I grieve with you. We become mothers and start loving our precious babies as soon as we know that they are growing inside of us. When we then suffer the death of our child in pregnancy, birth or infancy, we simply aren't prepared for the complete devastation of our hearts, dreams and lives.

I have lost five babies in pregnancy. I know right now you are sad, angry, numb, shocked, crushed, questioning, and may even be experiencing a few feelings that simply don't have names. You may have been taught that grief is five linear stages that you should process through and then it's complete. Forget that. Grief is messy and complex; there will be unexpected good days and there will be unexpected things that trigger waves of sadness that make it hard to breathe. Just be open to letting your thoughts and feelings out when possible.

If you are like me, your thoughts are probably re-living the events that preceded your loss over and over; re-thinking every choice and every decision you made that fateful day. What if I had only done ___? I ask you to beware letting your mind focus on the "what if." The "what if" is a dangerous question that all of us must face and learn to let go. What if I had stayed on progesterone longer or stopped it sooner? What if I had called the doctor sooner? What if I hadn't had that one cup of coffee two months ago? What if I hadn't had that sushi three years ago? The "what if" seeks to make meaning out of chaos, to find some reason that this horrible tragedy happened. But it attempts to find reason by blaming YOU, the one who loved your precious baby from her very first moment and did everything you reasonably could for her.

It is NOT your fault. You did the best you could with the information you had. You did nothing to deserve this tragedy. None of us are perfect, of course. But I can still assure you, that you did not deserve to lose your precious baby.

For all loss mothers, but most especially for those who may suffer multiple pregnancy losses like me, forgiving our bodies takes time. And regardless of whether we ever find a diagnosis, there will always be intrusive and impossible to answer questions that rise up about why this happened to us and how do we carry on with our lives. Please be gentle with yourself during this time. Allow yourself the freedom to grieve and to remember your child as you build a new life. Please try to surround yourself with people who will grieve with you and support you, whether in person or in an online community.

We will grieve with you, too.

Reen S.

http://community.babycenter.com/groups/a6745507/actively_trying_with_repeat_loss

"IT IS NOT YOUR FAULT. YOU DID THE BEST YOU COULD WITH THE INFORMATION YOU HAD. YOU DID NOTHING TO DESERVE THIS TRAGEDY."

DEAR BEAUTIFUL MAMA,

I'm sorry.

I'm sorry that we are meeting this way. I am sorry that you are reading this letter. I am sorry that I am writing it. I am sorry that you will go through the worst pain imaginable, and I am sorry that I know exactly what you are going through.

The most important thing that you need to know right now is THIS IS NOT YOUR FAULT. You will probably not believe me. I am not sure that I believe me. You will spend a lot of time questioning your actions during this pregnancy. Did that piece of chocolate have too much caffeine? Did you drink a glass of wine before you knew you were pregnant? Did you exercise too much or too little? Was that Benadryl pill really "safe" to take, even though your doctor said it was fine?

It was fine. You were fine. You were the best mother you could be to your child. Your baby felt every ounce of your love. You did not cause this to happen. Sometimes bad things happen for no reason.

I have walked in your shoes. My first child was stillborn one hour before my 37th week of pregnancy. My baby boy was moving one minute, and then he wasn't. There was no medical cause for his death; all the test results were normal. I will never know how he died. Sometimes the reason doesn't matter because the outcome is always the same.

The next few months will be excruciating. At first, you may be in shock and feel numb. You may spend hours crying. You may stay in bed all day. You may stop eating. Your body will act like every other woman who has had a baby and it will be confusing and sad. You won't know what day it is. You will wonder how your family and friends lives have continued while your life is stuck on pause.

You may wonder if you can do this, but you can. You can and you will because you do not have a choice. It will be the hardest thing that you have ever done, but you will do it with strength and courage. Losing your baby will forever be the worst day of your life. That means that every day following will be a tiny bit better. Your love for your child will keep you going.

Please take care of yourself. If all you do during the first month is get out of bed, take a shower and eat something, you are amazing. Just keep breathing. Take each day minute by minute.

You may find yourself lost in your grief and not able to understand your spouse or partner. Remember how much you love each other and how love created your child. This will be the most painful time in your life. Don't take your pain out on each other. Always remember the love.

I am deeply sorry for the loss of your baby.

—Renee

https://www.facebook.com/stephensheart

"JUST KEEP BREATHING. TAKE EACH DAY MINUTE BY MINUTE."

DEAR BROKEN MOMMA,

I am crying for you and me and all mommas who have to say goodbye to a child. This pain, this new life, is foreign territory and no matter how many have gone before you, the road is rocky and unpaved. Your pain is one of a kind, unique to you. Be whatever you need to be, sad, angry. Do not hide who are or how you feel.

Life will give you gifts, moments of peace, decent days, but you will always be inhabited by two parts. The joy and pain learn to coexist and you learn to accept the new you. You will see remnants of your old self, which you may not recognize or make you feel strange, as though you cannot quite recall how you were able to be that happy. Memories have a haze about them, one created by the knowledge that such deep sadness and pain exist. Go on. Keep moving. You have to, for you carry the memory of your child. Only you know what it is like to be his momma and to honor him through your life is a gift to him.

I pray for you, though we have never met, not by name but for all broken mommas who need to be blessed with purpose. Be kind to yourself.

With much Love and Prayers,

Stephanie DeBarbieris

Mom of Aaron

1/27/2014-5/13/2014

"LIFE WILL GIVE YOU GIFTS, MOMENTS OF PEACE, DECENT DAYS, BUT YOU WILL ALWAYS BE INHABITED BY TWO PARTS. THE JOY AND PAIN LEARN TO COEXIST AND YOU LEARN TO ACCEPT THE NEW YOU."

DEAREST MOMMA,

I feel with you. I feel your pain, your disbelief, your numbness. I feel your heart breaking into a million tiny, shattered pieces, unsure of how they will ever fit back together. I feel your confusion on your identity: Who are you now? Are you a mother since your child died in your womb? I feel you wondering: How can you grieve someone you never got the chance to know? How long will this pain last? Will you ever be yourself again?

I could tell you soon you will be yourself again; that things happen for a reason and this just wasn't meant to be. I could tell you that this is just God's (or nature's) way of tell you that there was something wrong with the child you carried. I could tell you not to worry, you will have another child soon enough; to not think about it and it will happen when you least expect it. I could tell you all you need is hope. But honestly that is all bullshit and I wish I could shield you from these comments because, trust me, you will receive your share.

What I will tell you is this: Yes, you are a mother. Yes, you will never be the same person you were before you conceived your child. The truth is that this your motherhood. You created life, you carried your child (no matter how brief) and for whatever reason your child couldn't stay. Life isn't fair and none of this will ever make sense. A year later as I write this to you, I am just as lost on this as I was day one. I'm not sure what I can tell you about normalcy because your view of it will change. Your new normal may be relearning how to find joy in the little things, reflecting, and allowing yourself to know it is ok to laugh and dream again. I can tell you the tears will not flow as frequently, but they don't magically disappear. I can tell you will have moments where you feel very much alone, where others in your life will not understand your grief and why you can't move on.

But the truth is you are moving on. Living is moving on. Your child was and is still a part of you and it is ok to remember them. Living life doesn't mean your child can't have a place in it. Talk about them and to them, create your own rituals, and do what feels right in your heart. I cannot stress that enough. Don't punish yourself for not fitting into someone else's view of grief and healing. They are not you and they are not your child's mother; only you can be that and that in itself is precious.

Momma, even if you don't see it now I know this; you are a strong woman, one of the strongest.

In love and support,

Stephanie

Erryn Shiloh's Mother
Little boy born to Heaven 10.9.14

"LIVING IS MOVING ON. YOUR CHILD WAS AND IS STILL A PART OF YOU AND IT IS OK TO REMEMBER THEM. LIVING LIFE DOESN'T MEAN YOUR CHILD CAN'T HAVE A PLACE IN IT."

IN THE END, SWEET MOTHER, HERE IS WHAT I WANT YOU TO KNOW:

You are a beautiful mother. It takes bravery and courage and profound love to mother a child you cannot see or hold or touch.

You are strong. Whether you feel strong or not, you are. Even when you are on your knees in tears. Even when you wish you could have just left this earth with your baby. Even when the best you can do is simply drag yourself out of bed. Even in your darkest moments, you are strong.

It takes courage and bravery to mother as we do. To love that which we cannot see or touch is beauty in action. To love beyond death is magnificent.

You are magnificent.

Believe that there is a light beyond this aching darkness. You probably can't see that light yet and you don't have to. I am here holding that light for you. There are many of us here, having lived what you are living. You don't have to know the way. We know it for you.

Just take one step, and then another.

When you can't take a step, it's ok to crawl.

When crawling is too much, it's ok to take a rest.

You will get up again.

You will find your way through this darkness of grief and loss and pain.

There is no rush to this journey.

They will be your babies for always. You are a mother for life.

Not even death can take that away.

You love, beautiful mother. You love hard and fierce and deep. This is your greatest gift. Your love will carry you through this deepest sorrow.

Your love will become your light.

Love on, sweet mother, and love always.

xoxo,

Emily

(an excerpt from the "Invisible Mothers: When Love Doesn't Die" book)

"YOU LOVE, BEAUTIFUL MOTHER. YOU LOVE HARD AND FIERCE AND DEEP. THIS IS YOUR GREATEST GIFT. YOUR LOVE WILL CARRY YOU THROUGH THIS DEEPEST SORROW."

WHERE YOU CAN FIND US

Finally, if you get nothing else from this book, know that we are with you and you are not alone. Here are a few of the many places you may find us. Join us and let us support you.

Websites and Blogs

www.emilyrlong.com

www.stillmothers.com

www.stillstandingmag.com

www.walkingwithelliot.com

www.hopeintheheartache.wordpress.com

http://aboutholland.wordpress.com

www.loveisdeeperstill.blogspot.com

http://mommamighty.wordpress.com

https://babylossmama.wordpress.com

www.expectingthunexpectedblog.wordpress.com

https://jeniferruby.wordpress.com

www.gpshope.org

http://healinggracebirthsupport.com/

https://pregnancyafterlosssupport.com/

http://www.loridoesmd.blogspot.com/

Facebook Groups/Pages or Online Forums

www.facebook.com/InvisibleMothers

www.facebook.com/StillStandingMag

www.facebook.com/AllThatLoveCanDo/

www.facebook.com/stephensheart

www.facebook.com/loveisdeeperstill

http://community.babycenter.com/groups/a6745507/actively_trying_with_repeat_loss

FB - GPS Hope: Grieving Parents Sharing Hope

www.facebook.com/hgracedoulas